Hercules

STARTER LEVEL   250 HEADWORDS

OXFORD
UNIVERSITY PRESS

Great Clarendon Street, Oxford OX2 6DP

Oxford University Press is a department of the University of Oxford.
It furthers the University's objective of excellence in research, scholarship,
and education by publishing worldwide in

Oxford New York

Auckland Cape Town Dar es Salaam Hong Kong Karachi
Kuala Lumpur Madrid Melbourne Mexico City Nairobi
New Delhi Shanghai Taipei Toronto

With offices in

Argentina Austria Brazil Chile Czech Republic France Greece
Guatemala Hungary Italy Japan Poland Portugal Singapore
South Korea Switzerland Thailand Turkey Ukraine Vietnam

OXFORD and OXFORD ENGLISH are registered trade marks of
Oxford University Press in the UK and in certain other countries

ISBN: 978 0 19 424715 3 Book
ISBN: 978 0 19 463926 2 Book and Audio Pack

Printed in China

This book is printed on paper from certified and well-managed sources.

ACKNOWLEDGEMENTS

Illustrations and cover by: Janos Jantner

DOMINOES

Series Editors: Bill Bowler and Sue Parminter

Hercules

Retold by Janet Hardy-Gould

Illustrated by Janos Jantner

Janet Hardy-Gould has worked as a teacher of English for many years. In her free time she enjoys reading history books and modern novels, visiting other European countries, and drinking tea with her friends. She lives in the ancient town of Lewes in the south of England with her husband, Geoff, and two children, Gabriella and Joseph. She has written a number of books for students of English, including *Henry VIII and his Six Wives* and *King Arthur* in the Oxford Bookworms series, and *The Great Fire of London, Mulan, Sinbad* and *The Travels of Ibn Battuta* in the Dominoes series.

OXFORD
UNIVERSITY PRESS

BEFORE READING

1 **In the story, Hercules does different things. Match the first and the second parts of the sentences. Use a dictionary to help you.**

1 some apples.

2 a big lion.

a Hercules kills ...   **b** Hercules runs after ...

3 some dirty stables.

4 a very quick deer.

c Hercules goes to a far away garden and gets ...   **d** Hercules cleans ...

2 **Who helps Hercules? Tick two boxes.**

a ☐ King Eurystheus   **b** ☐ the goddess Athena   **c** ☐ the goddess Hera

d ☐ King Creon   **e** ☐ Iolaus   **f** ☐ Princess Admete

▣ CHAPTER 1 ▣

One day, in her **palace** in Greece, **Princess** Alcmene has a son. She calls the boy Hercules.

'What a big, **strong** boy!' say Alcmene's friends when they see him.

'Of course he's big and strong,' smiles Alcmene. 'His father's Zeus, **king** of the **gods**.'

But not everybody likes Hercules. The **goddess** Hera is looking through the palace window. Hera is Zeus's **wife** – and she's far from happy.

'When I see that boy,' says Hera, 'I remember his mother, Alcmene. Why does Zeus always run after different women? It's not right. I'm his wife! He never thinks of me!'

She leaves Alcmene's palace angrily.

palace a big house where a king lives

princess the daughter of a king

strong with a body that works well

king the most important man in a country

god an important being who never dies and who decides what happens in the world

goddess a woman god

wife a woman living with a man

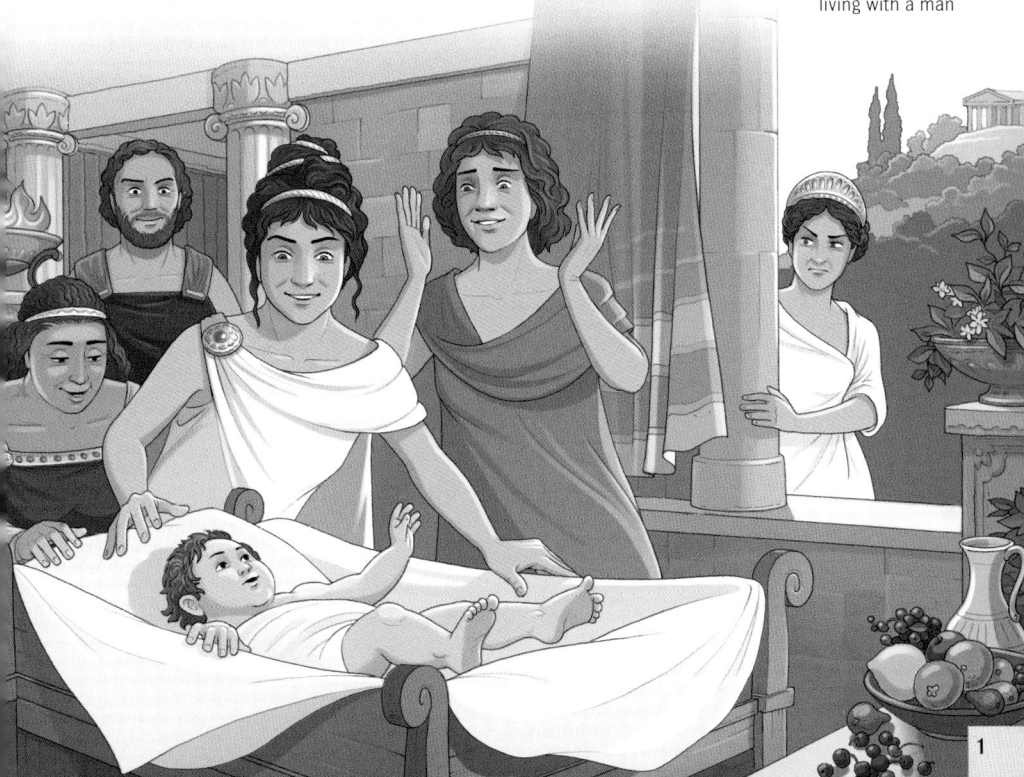

1

Some nights later, Hera comes back – and she puts two big **snakes** in Hercules's bed. 'Goodbye, little boy!' she laughs.

But when Hera comes back next morning, Hercules is alive. He has the dead snakes in his hands.

'Grrr!' cries Hera angrily. 'You wait. I'm watching you, Hercules. You can't get away from me!'

Later, when Hercules is older, he has many teachers. They come to the palace and teach him there. But he is not a very good student. He doesn't find it easy to learn, and he is often angry when he can't understand things.

In the end, Alcmene **sends** Hercules away to some hills in the country near Thebes. He feels better there. He can run through the trees

snake a long animal with no legs

send to make someone go somewhere

happily for hours, and there are **lions** for him to **fight**. Soon after he arrives, some people come to the hills because they want to take the King of Thebes's **cows**, but Hercules stops them.

When King Creon of Thebes hears about Hercules, he speaks to his daughter.

'Megara,' he says, 'Hercules is a good strong young man. Would you like to **marry** him?'

'Yes, Father,' answers Megara.

So Creon's men go and speak to Hercules, and he comes to Thebes and marries Megara. Soon they have three sons.

Hercules is happy with his beautiful wife and his young sons. But Hera is angry. 'Alcmene's son is doing well,' she says. 'I must change that.'

lion a big yellow animal with long brown hair round its face

fight to hit again and again

cow an animal that gives milk

marry to make someone your husband or wife

3

Very early one morning – when Hercules, Megara and their sons are in their beds – Hera sends a black **cloud** over Hercules's head. He opens his eyes, but he can't see a thing through the cloud. Suddenly there are four men in black in front of him. They want to kill Megara and the boys. 'I must stop them,' thinks Hercules. He fights the men and kills them one by one. Then he goes back to sleep. Later, when he opens his eyes, there are no men there, only his wife and sons. But their bodies are cold, and they do not move or speak. Suddenly Hercules feels afraid.

'Oh, no!' he cries. 'My wife and sons are dead! And I'm their killer. It's the work of one of the gods. He – or she – is angry with me!'

Hercules goes to King Creon and says, 'The gods are angry with me. Help me!'

'Very well,' says Creon. 'What's the matter?'

Hercules tells Creon everything. The king's face is white when he hears about his daughter and his grandsons.

'Leave my palace at once,' says Creon. 'I can do nothing for you. Go to Delphi and talk to the **priestess** there. Perhaps she can help.'

At Delphi, the priestess tells Hercules: 'It's a very bad **crime** when a man kills his wife and sons. So you're right. The gods *are* angry with you.'

cloud a big white or grey thing in the sky

priestess a woman who works in a temple

crime killing someone, or doing something very bad

'I know that, but what can I do about it?' asks Hercules.

'For twelve years you must work for King Eurystheus, and do twelve **tasks** for him,' says the priestess. 'When you finish, the gods can **forgive** your crime.'

'Oh no! Not my **cousin** Eurystheus!' thinks Hercules. 'He doesn't like me because I'm bigger and stronger than him. And now I'm working for him!'

Hercules goes to King Eurystheus and tells him about the twelve tasks.

'All right, Hercules!' smiles Eurystheus coldly. 'I have a first task for you. There's a big, hungry lion in Nemea. It's eating everybody there! Kill it, and bring its dead body back to me.'

Hercules leaves Eurystheus's palace at once.

'Good luck with your first – and last – task, Hercules,' laughs the king.

Just then, the goddess Hera arrives.

'Good work, Eurystheus. Hercules is a dead man, I think,' she laughs. 'No one can fight that lion and get away alive.'

task work

forgive to stop being angry with someone after they do something bad

cousin the son (or daughter) of your mother's (or father's) sister (or brother)

READING CHECK

Choose the correct words to complete the sentences.

a When Hercules is a young boy, he's very ill/strong.

b Hercules is Princess Alcmene's/the goddess Hera's son.

c The god Zeus is Hercules's brother/father.

d The goddess Hera/god Zeus is very angry with Hercules.

e Hercules finds/doesn't find it easy to learn new things with his teacher.

f When Hercules goes and lives in the hills, he is very happy/angry.

g Hercules leaves/kills his wife and sons.

h Hercules must work for King Eurystheus and do ten/twelve things for him.

i King Eurystheus is Hercules's cousin/friend.

j Hercules must go to Nemea and kill a snake/lion.

WORD WORK

1 Find eleven more words from Chapter 1 in the wordsquare.

f	o	r	g	i	v	e	z	k	w
i	l	q	f	o	m	u	p	s	i
g	m	a	r	r	y	w	r	b	f
h	y	t	a	s	k	j	i	x	e
t	i	s	b	v	w	p	e	f	j
c	m	t	j	c	o	u	s	i	n
r	p	r	x	l	m	i	t	b	r
i	q	o	m	o	z	s	e	n	d
m	k	n	r	u	h	n	s	q	c
e	j	g	o	d	d	e	s	s	v

ACTIVITIES

2 Use the words from Activity 1 to complete the sentences.

a 'You're two hours late!' 'We're very sorry! Please .forgive.. us!'

b 'Let's go in now. It's cold out here and there's a big dark .... in the sky over there.'

c 'Please don't .... me away to the country. I want to stay here.'

d 'What are you reading?' 'It's a book about a very bad .... : two men take a lot of money from a shop.'

e 'I have a little .... for you. Can you go to the supermarket and buy some bread?'

f 'We're learning about the Greek .... Hera at the moment.'

g 'Mr Black is my .... – his father is my father's brother. And that woman is his .... , Mrs Black.'

h 'I love you. Please .... me, Juliet!' 'Yes, of course, Romeo!'

i Hercules asks the .... at Delphi for help.

j 'That man is very big and .... Everybody is afraid of him and nobody wants to .... him.'

3 Match the words with the pictures.

cow   king   lion   palace   princess   snake

d ....

a ..lion......

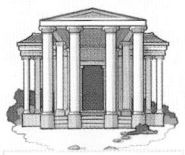
b ....

c ....

e ....

GUESS WHAT

What happens in the next chapter? Tick one box.

a ☐ Hercules fights and kills Hera.

b ☐ Hercules fights and kills the lion.

c ☐ The lion runs after Hercules and eats his arm.

d ☐ The lion likes Hercules and is his new friend.

f ....

7

🔲 CHAPTER 2 🔲

arrow you shoot things with this

skin the outside of an animal's body

sword a long, sharp knife for fighting

jar something that you can put things in, for example a jar of oil

monster an animal that is very bad to look at

lake a lot of water with land round it

Hercules goes to Nemea and finds the lion, but it's sleeping when he arrives. 'I can kill it with one or two **arrows**,' he thinks. But his arrows don't go through the lion's **skin.** So then he hits the lion on the head with his **sword**. But the lion only opens one eye and goes back to sleep. In the end, Hercules kills the lion with his hands, and after that he takes off its skin. He quickly puts the lion's skin over his head and back. 'When I wear this, no arrows or swords can kill me,' he says happily. He then runs back to the king's palace. Eurystheus is very afraid when he sees Hercules and he quickly gets into a big brown **jar**.

'There's a **monster** with nine heads in the **Lake** of Lerna,' cries Eurystheus from the jar. 'People call it the Hydra. Your task number two is to go and kill it!'

Near the palace, Hercules meets his young cousin, Iolaus. 'I can't stop and talk,' says Hercules. 'I'm going to the Lake of Lerna. I must kill the Hydra there.'

'Can I come too?' asks Iolaus excitedly.

When they arrive at the lake, it is nearly dark. Hercules puts some **fire** onto an arrow and **shoots** it over the water. 'I want to call the Hydra to me!' he says.

Suddenly the nine heads of the Hydra come out of the lake. They look at Iolaus and Hercules with angry red eyes.

'Help!' cries Iolaus.

fire this is red and hot, and it burns

shoot to send something quickly far away; to hit something from far away

cut off to take a little thing away from a bigger thing with a knife

stump the thing that stays behind after you cut off a head, arm or leg

against to think badly of someone, and so make bad things happen to them

burn to make something hot with fire

golden the colour of, or made of, an expensive yellow metal

deer a large animal that can run fast

catch to take quickly in your hands

Hercules quickly takes out his sword and **cuts off** one of the Hydra's heads. But from the red **stump** come two more new heads. Hercules then cuts off a different head, and again two more new heads come from that stump.

'Oh, no!' he thinks.

Just then, the goddess Athena arrives. 'I come from your father, Zeus,' she says. 'He is angry with the goddess Hera because she is working **against** you. He wants to help you with your tasks. What can I do for you?'

'How can I kill the Hydra?' asks Hercules. 'Tell me quickly!'

'When you cut off the heads, you must **burn** the stumps. No new heads can come from them after that. Good luck!'

So Hercules cuts off the monster's heads one by one and Iolaus burns the stumps. When Hercules cuts off the last head, the Hydra suddenly goes down in the water and dies.

The next morning, Hercules arrives back at the palace, but he can't find the king. 'Eurystheus!' he calls. 'I'm here! The Hydra's dead!'

'All right, I can hear you,' says Eurystheus, and he comes out angrily from his big brown jar. 'For your third task you must find the goddess Artemis's **golden deer** and bring it back here. That deer can run faster than any arrow. Nobody can **catch** it.'

Hercules finds the golden deer and he runs after it for a year and a day. The deer runs up hills, down hills, and across the country, but Hercules can't catch it. One day, Hercules sees the beautiful deer next to a lake. It is drinking quietly from the water. Hercules catches it and runs back to the palace with the deer in his arms.

'King Eurystheus! I have something for you!' cries Hercules. 'Come and see!'

Eurystheus comes out of the palace with his daughter, Admete. Hercules puts the golden deer in front of Eurystheus. But before the king can take the deer, it runs away.

'I want that golden deer!' cries Admete. 'And when I want something, I always get it.'

'Not this time,' says Eurystheus and he looks angrily at Hercules. 'Task number four is to go into the **mountains** and catch a big **wild boar** there. And you must bring it back alive!'

mountain a big hill

wild boar a big pig with long black hair on it that lives in the country

READING CHECK

Match the two parts of the sentences.

a Hercules takes and wears ...   1 a lake.

b Eurystheus is afraid and jumps into ...   2 the lion's skin.

c The Hydra lives in ...   3 the golden deer.

d The god Zeus is angry with ...   4 an arrow.

e The goddess Athena helps ...   5 a big brown jar.

f Iolaus and Hercules kill ...   6 Hercules and Iolaus.

g The golden deer can run faster than ...   7 the goddess Hera.

h Admete is angry because she wants ...   8 a big wild boar.

i Hercules must go in the mountains to catch ...   9 the Hydra.

WORD WORK

1 These words don't match the pictures. Correct them.

a ~~arrow~~ ....deer....   b monster ....   c jar ....

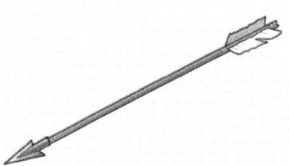

d lake ....   e deer ....   f stump ....

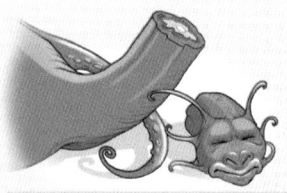

g wild boar ....   h mountain ....

12

2 Find eight more words from the story in the Hydra.

goldencatchesswordskinfirecutsoffburnshootsagainst

3 Use the words from Activity 2 to complete these sentences about the story.

a Hercules .cuts..off. the Hydra's heads with his big ……………..

b Eurystheus is very afraid when he sees Hercules with the lion's …………… over his head.

c After a year and a day, Hercules …………… the beautiful …………… deer and takes it back to the palace.

d Hercules puts some …………… onto an arrow. He then …………… the arrow over the water and the Hydra comes out of the lake.

e The goddess Hera is very angry and she is working …………… Hercules.

f The goddess Athena speaks to Hercules and Iolaus. Iolaus then begins to …………… the stumps of the Hydra's heads.

GUESS WHAT

What happens in the next chapter? Tick the boxes.

	Yes	No
a Hercules comes back to the palace with the big wild boar.	☐	☐
b Hercules can't catch the wild boar and Eurystheus is very happy.	☐	☐
c The wild boar comes into the palace and runs after Princess Admete.	☐	☐
d Hercules cleans out some dirty old stables for King Augeas.	☐	☐
e Hercules makes a beautiful new palace for King Augeas.	☐	☐

▣ CHAPTER 3 ▣

huge very big

rock a very big stone

chase to run after something or someone

snow something soft, cold and white

top the highest part of something

Hercules runs up into the cold mountains. Suddenly he looks up and sees a **huge** wild boar on a **rock** near him.

Hercules stops and thinks for a minute. Then he **chases** the wild boar up into the **snow** at the **top** of the mountain. The wild boar has little legs and it can't run very easily through the snow.

Hercules catches the wild boar. He puts it on his back and walks down the mountain.

Soon Hercules arrives at the palace. King Eurystheus looks at the huge wild boar on Hercules's back and gets quickly into his jar again. 'Take it away!' he cries.

Hercules comes back not long after without the wild boar. 'For your next task you need to visit King Augeas. He has some interesting work for you,' says Eurystheus. 'He has hundreds of **bulls** and nobody **cleans** their dirty **stables**. You must clean them all in one day!'

▣

Hercules meets King Augeas at the stables and he tells the king about his task.

'But nobody can clean those dirty stables in one day!' laughs the king. 'Look at them!'

Hercules looks through the door of the stables and he doesn't feel very happy.

'They're very dirty, it's true!' he says.

▣

Just then, on a hill behind the stables, Hercules sees a **river** with big rocks next to it. He walks up to the river and sits down on one of the rocks. 'I need to think carefully about this,' he says to Augeas.

bull a male cow

clean to stop something being dirty

stable a building where horses or other animals sleep at night

river water that moves in a long line

15

The next morning, Hercules gets up early. First he takes the bulls out of the stable and away up the hill. After that, he makes a big **hole** in the **wall** at one **end** of the stables, and he makes a second hole in the wall at the **other** end of the stables. He then takes the rocks from next to the river and puts them into the water one by one. Hercules works all morning. 'What are you doing?' asks King Augeas.

'Wait and see!' says Hercules.

🔲

Hercules is slowly making a big wall of rocks across the river! When he finishes the wall, the water in the river has nowhere to go. After some time the water suddenly comes out of the river and it runs down the hill to the stables. The water then goes quickly through the dirty stables and it cleans them beautifully.

That evening, Hercules takes all the rocks out of the river and the water doesn't go down the hill through the stables any more. He then takes some small rocks and closes the two big holes in the stable walls before the bulls come back in for the night.

🔲

When King Augeas sees the clean stables, he is very happy. 'Please stay and eat at my palace tonight!' he says.

🔲

The next morning, Hercules arrives back at Eurystheus's palace with a big smile on his face. 'I don't want to hear about the stables!' says Eurystheus angrily. He doesn't get into his jar this time. 'Now, for task number six, you must go to Lake Stymphalus. There are some big birds there, and they are killing all the cows. You must stop them!'

hole an opening in something

wall something long, strong, and tall that is made of rocks; the side of a building

end where something finishes

other different

READING CHECK

Correct the mistakes in these sentences.

a Hercules catches the boar in the ~~river~~ *snow* at the top of the mountain.

b When Eurystheus sees the wild boar, he jumps into his bed.

c Hercules needs to clean out the stables in one week.

d A lot of horses live in the stables.

e Hercules cleans the stables with water from a lake.

f Hercules makes a big hole in the door of the stables.

g King Augeus is very angry when he sees the stables.

h Hercules must go and find the little birds at Lake Stymphalus.

i The birds are killing a lot of people.

WORD WORK

1 Find words in the jars to complete the sentences.

 tehro
 gehu
 vrrie
 alwsl

a 'This photo is good but that o±ber photo is better.'

b 'He lives in a h_ _ _ house with forty rooms.'

c 'It's raining and there's a lot of water in the r_ _ _ _.'

d 'The w_ _ _ _ of my bedroom are blue.'

 laenc
 osrkc
 lubls
 nwso pto

e 'Your shoes are dirty.' 'Yes, I must c_ _ _ _ them.'

f 'Be careful in the sea there are r_ _ _ _ under the water.'

g 'Look, there are some cows.' 'They aren't cows; they're b_ _ _ _!'

h 'There's always s_ _ _ at the t_ of that mountain.'

leho

ned

tbssael

i 'Oh no! There's a h_ _ _ in my trousers.'

j 'My house is at the e_ _ of the street.'

k 'At night the horses go into the s_ _ _ _ _ _.'

GUESS WHAT

In the next chapter Hercules meets:

some birds

a white bull

some horses.

They are not very nice! Look at the pictures below. Tick the boxes.

a The birds kill cows with their ...

1 ☐

2 ☐

3 ☐

b When the white bull opens its mouth, ... comes out.

1 ☐

2 ☐

3 ☐

c The horses eat ...

1 ☐

2 ☐

3 ☐

A t Lake Stymphalus, Hercules meets some men from the small town near there. 'Please help us, Hercules!' they say. 'There are huge birds in the tall trees next to the lake. They have **metal feathers**. From time to time they leave the trees for the sky, and then they **drop** their feathers down on our cows and kill them.'

Hercules looks up just then and sees hundreds of birds in the sky over his head. The birds suddenly begin to drop their metal feathers down on him. But the feathers can't go through Hercules's lion skin. He shoots lots of arrows at the birds, but they quickly fly away up into the tops of the tall trees again.

'I can't shoot them up there,' thinks Hercules. 'Athena! Where are you? I need help!'

metal something hard and bright; gold is an expensive metal

feathers birds have these on their bodies

drop to let something go down quickly, sometimes not wanting to do it

Just then, Athena arrives with a large metal **rattle** in her hand. 'You can make a big noise with this,' she says. 'Those birds don't like a lot of noise, you see!' And with that, she gives the rattle to Hercules.

rattle this makes a noise when you move it

Hercules puts the rattle up over his head and moves it left and right again and again. It makes a lot of noise. Suddenly the birds fly down out of the trees. Hercules can then easily shoot and kill them with his arrows.

Hercules goes back to the palace. 'Eurystheus, I have a bird from Lake Stymphalus for you,' he calls, and he puts the dead bird down not far from Eurystheus's jar.

'Let's see,' says Eurystheus, and he comes out of his jar. He goes over and looks at the dead bird – and he cuts his hand on one of its metal feathers. 'Hercules, get out of here!' cries the king angrily. 'For task number seven you must go at once to Crete and catch King Minos's white bull there. And be quick about it!'

Hercules goes by **boat** to Crete. When he arrives there, King Minos is very happy to see him. 'There's a big white bull,' he says. 'It's running here and there and killing people everywhere. You're big and strong, Hercules. Please catch it and take it away. It's in a small town near here now.'

Hercules goes to the town and waits. It is very quiet there and nobody is on the streets. Suddenly the bull comes out from behind a tree and it runs towards Hercules. The bull has big **horns** and fire is coming out of its mouth. The bull comes nearer and nearer to Hercules but the fire doesn't burn him because he's wearing his lion skin. Hercules takes the bull by the horns and gets up on its back.

For two days the bull runs all over Crete. Hercules stays on its back day and night. In the end, the bull is very tired and it can't run – or fight – any more. Hercules quickly puts the bull on his boat, and takes it back to King Eurystheus.

Eurystheus is very afraid of the bull. 'I don't want that thing in my home! Kill it at once!' he cries from his jar. But Hercules opens the palace door, and the bull runs away.

That night Eurystheus talks to the goddess Hera. 'Hercules does all our tasks very easily,' he says. 'What can we find for him to do next?'

Hera thinks for a minute; then she smiles. 'I know!' she cries, and she says something quietly in the king's ear. 'Oh, yes,' he laughs. 'That's good! That's very good!'

The next morning Eurystheus calls for Hercules. When Hercules arrives, the king is sitting in his big metal chair. 'Hercules,' he says. 'Task number eight is to bring back the horses from the palace of King Diomedes.'

'Of course,' smiles Hercules, and he walks quickly out of the palace.

'And don't forget,' begins Hera, and she looks out from behind Eurystheus's chair, 'Diomedes's horses eat people!'

Then she and Eurystheus begin to laugh and laugh. But Hercules is far away from them now, and he doesn't hear.

Hercules goes by boat to the palace of King Diomedes with four of his friends. 'We're tired, hungry and far from home,' they say to the king when they arrive at his door.

'Come in!' says King Diomedes. 'You can eat with us this evening and stay here tonight.' He looks at the men's big, strong bodies and he thinks: 'I can give them to my hungry horses tomorrow.'

That evening, Hercules hears King Diomedes talk quietly to one of his men. 'When Hercules and his friends are sleeping tonight, you must help me to kill them,' the king says to the man. 'They can be a nice breakfast for my horses!'

Hercules says nothing. But later he talks to his friends. 'They want to kill us tonight! We can't go to sleep. We must wait for them, and fight them when they come for us.'

That night Hercules's friends go to sleep very quickly, but Hercules cannot sleep. Suddenly King Diomedes and his men come into the room. 'Quick! Get out of bed!' cries Hercules to his friends. They get up, fight, and kill the king and his men.

'What shall we do with the dead bodies, Hercules?' ask his friends.

'Give them to the horses, of course!' he answers.

The horses are very quiet and happy after they eat Diomedes and his men.

When Hercules brings the horses back to Eurystheus's palace they look hungrily at the king.

'Take those horses away!' cries Eurystheus. He runs into the garden and goes behind a tree.

When Hercules comes back without the horses, Princess Admete is talking to her father. '**Queen** Hippolyta of the Amazons has a beautiful golden **belt**,' she says. 'And I want it!'

'Well, that's your next task, Hercules!' says Eurystheus from behind the tree. 'Task number nine: get Queen Hippolyta's belt, and bring it back for my daughter!'

queen the most important woman in a country

belt you wear this round your middle

READING CHECK

Are these sentences true or false? Tick the boxes.

		True	False
a	The birds kill the cows with small rocks.	☐	☑
b	Athena gives Hercules a metal sword.	☐	☐
c	The birds fly out of the trees because Hercules makes a big noise.	☐	☐
d	Hercules kills the birds with his hands.	☐	☐
e	Eurystheus is angry because he cuts his hand on a metal feather.	☐	☐
f	The white bull is running all over Crete and killing people.	☐	☐
g	Hercules gets on the bull's back and stays there for two hours.	☐	☐
h	Hercules knows all about Diomedes's horses before he does task eight.	☐	☐
i	Diomedes wants to kill Hercules and his men when they are sleeping.	☐	☐
j	The horses eat the dead bodies of Diomedes and his men.	☐	☐

WORD WORK

1 Find words from Chapter 4 to match the pictures.

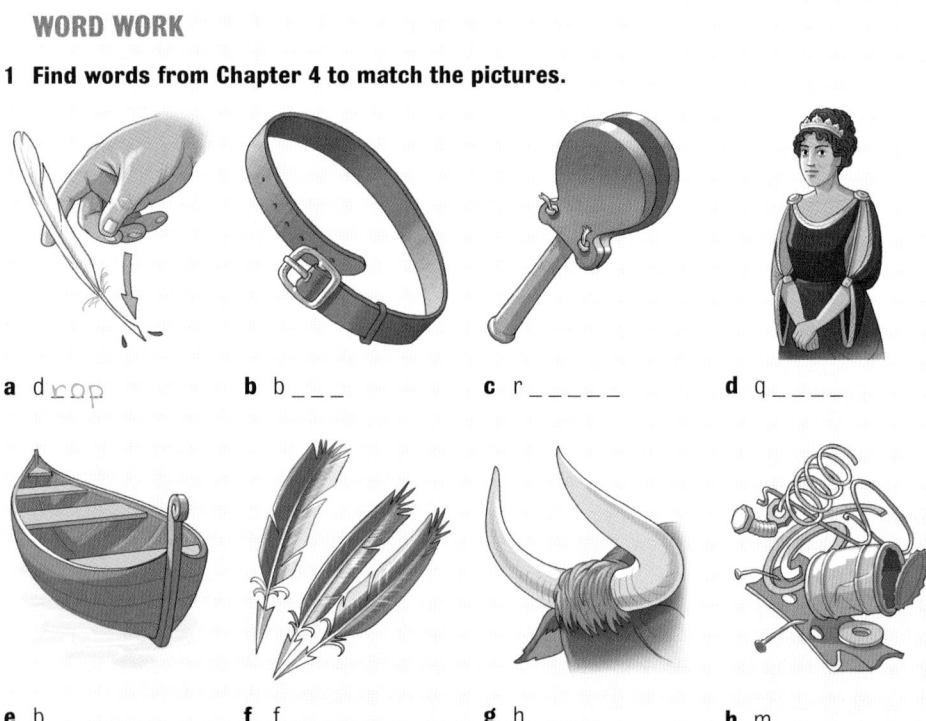

a d r o p

b b _ _ _

c r _ _ _ _ _

d q _ _ _ _

e b _ _ _

f f _ _ _ _ _ _ _

g h _ _ _ _

h m _ _ _ _

2 Match the words from Activity 1 with the definitions.

a to send something down quickly from your hand, perhaps when you don't want to ....drop....

b you can go across a river or a lake in this ....

c bulls have two of these white things on their heads ....

d a very young child can play with this; it makes a noise when you move it ....

e men sometimes wear this at the top of their trousers ....

f the most important woman in a country; the wife of a king ....

g something hard and bright, like gold ....

h because birds have these on their bodies they can stay warm ....

GUESS WHAT

Hercules goes to the country of the Amazons to get Queen Hippolyta's belt. Who wants to stop Hercules? Tick one box.

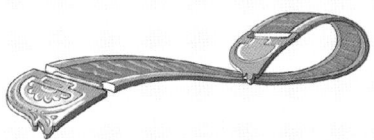

a ☐ Queen Hippolyta

b ☐ Princess Admete

c ☐ the goddess Hera

d ☐ a monster with three heads

CHAPTER 5

So Hercules goes by boat to the country of the Amazons. He takes some friends with him. 'We must be careful,' says Hercules when they arrive. 'Only big strong women live here, and they usually kill men when they meet them, people say.'

Hercules soon finds Queen Hippolyta. She is tall, strong, and very beautiful. He is **surprised** when Hippolyta is nice to him. 'Hello, Hercules,' she says. 'It's wonderful to meet you. You're the strongest man in the **world**, I hear.'

'Thank you,' smiles Hercules. With his sword he quickly cuts two Hs and an arrow of love between them on a tree. Then he takes some flowers in his hand, and he gives them to the Amazon Queen.

surprised feeling that something very new is suddenly happening

world where we all live; people live in lots of different countries in the world

'Thank you!' says Hippolyta.

Hercules then tells Hippolyta about his task. 'I need to take your golden belt back to King Eurystheus's daughter,' he says.

'You can have it, of course,' says Hippolyta, and at once she puts her hands on her beautiful belt.

But Hera is watching all this from behind a tree. 'This task is going well for Hercules,' she thinks. 'I must do something fast and stop him.'

So Hera puts on the dress of an Amazon woman and she goes and talks to Hippolyta's **guards**. 'Hercules wants to take Queen Hippolyta's belt and then kill her,' says Hera.

The guards run quickly to their queen. She is giving Hercules the golden belt. 'Stop!' they cry. Hercules quickly takes the belt. The guards fight Hercules and his friends, but in the end they get away from the Amazons and back to their boat – and Hercules has the belt with him!

Hercules is very tired when he arrives back at the palace. 'Where's that belt?' asks Princess Admete. She puts it on. 'Oh, no! I can't wear that,' she says angrily. 'It's huge!'

guard someone or something that stops people from killing a king or queen

Hercules goes into the palace garden, sits down, and closes his eyes. Eurystheus puts his head up from behind some flowers. 'What are you doing here, Hercules? he says. 'You have three more tasks to do! First find Geryon, the monster with three heads, and bring back his red cows to me.'

Geryon lives in a far away country, and Hercules goes by boat across dark and angry seas to get there. When he arrives, he gets off his boat and looks everywhere. He can see the red cows on a hill, but he can't see Geryon. 'This is an easy task,' he thinks. 'I can put those cows on my boat this minute and go home at once.'

Suddenly Geryon walks over the hill. He has three huge heads and six long arms. Hercules quickly goes behind a rock. 'Who's there?' cries the monster. 'Come out, now!'

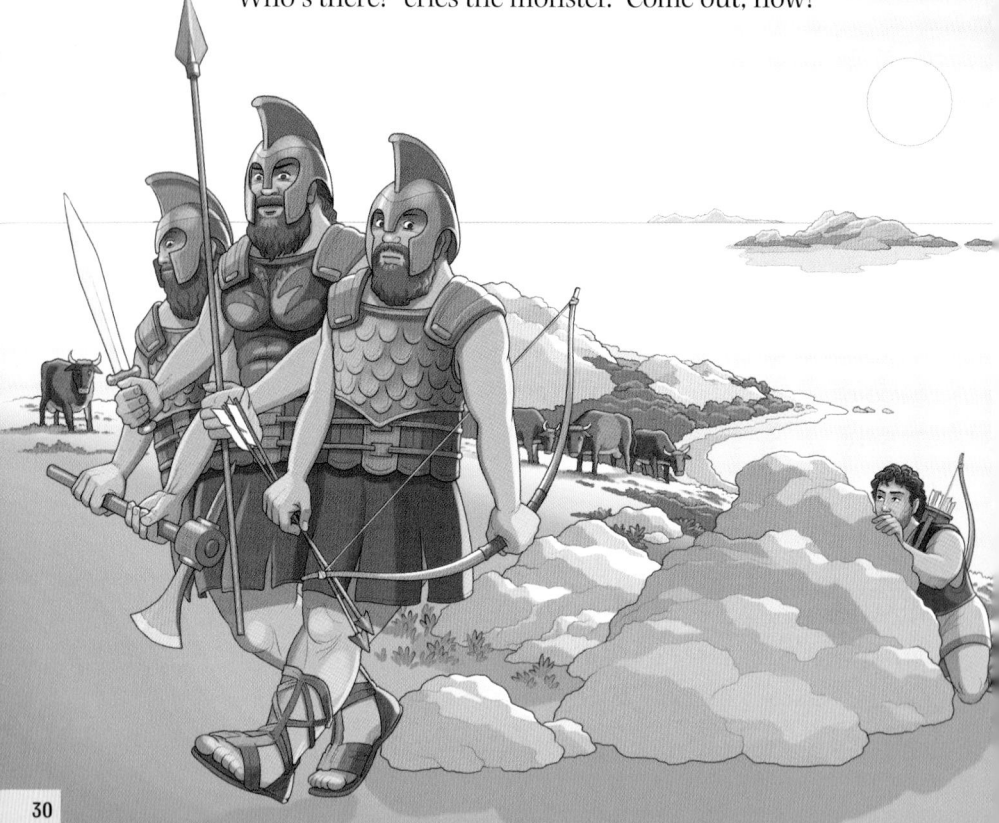

Hercules thinks quietly for a minute or two. Then he runs out and stands behind Geryon. 'I'm behind you!' he calls.

Geryon slowly moves his three big heads to look down at Hercules. Hercules then shoots one arrow through all three of the monster's heads, and at once Geryon **falls** dead at his feet.

Hercules puts all Geryon's cows on his boat, and goes home with them. When he brings them into the palace garden, they start to eat all the flowers there.

'Take those big fat cows out of my garden!' calls Eurystheus from a palace window.

Hercules takes the cows away.

'You must go to the end of the world now, and look for the goddess Hera's garden there!' cries Eurystheus when Hercules comes back. 'And bring me three golden apples from the garden, once you find it.'

When Hercules leaves the palace, Hera and Eurystheus laugh for a long time. 'Only gods can go into my garden,' cries Hera in the end. 'And Hercules is only a man. He can never take those golden apples from the tree! And of course, there's my friendly **dragon** in the garden, too! Ha, ha, ha!'

fall to go down suddenly

dragon a big animal that can fly through the sky and send fire from its mouth

READING CHECK

Choose the right words to finish the sentences.

a In the country of the Amazons there are only ...

  1 ☐ tall angry men.

  2 ☑ big strong women.

  3 ☐ small young women.

b When Hippolyta first meets Hercules she is ... him.

  1 ☐ afraid of

  2 ☐ angry with

  3 ☐ nice to

c Hera wants to stop Hercules so she talks to ...

  1 ☐ Queen Hippolyta's guards.

  2 ☐ Queen Hippolyta.

  3 ☐ Hercules's friends.

d Hercules and his friends ... with Hippolyta's guards.

  1 ☐ fight

  2 ☐ laugh

  3 ☐ eat dinner

e Princess Admete is ... with the belt.

  1 ☐ careful

  2 ☐ happy

  3 ☐ not happy

f Geryon is a huge ... with six arms.

  1 ☐ god

  2 ☐ man

  3 ☐ monster

g Hercules shoots an arrow through Geryon's ...

  1 ☐ heads.

  2 ☐ arms.

  3 ☐ legs.

h The red cows eat the ... in the palace garden.

  1 ☐ trees

  2 ☐ flowers

  3 ☐ birds

WORD WORK

1 Find four more words from Chapter 5 in the sword.

hafalldragondguardworldesurpriseds

2 Use the words to complete the sentences on page 33.

ACTIVITIES

a 'The king is afraid of people so he always has a ...*guard*... in front of his door.'

b 'What is the longest river in the ....?' 'It's the Nile in Africa.'

c 'He doesn't usually come to school on Fridays.' 'Yes, I'm .... to see him today.'

d 'I like that children's book ; it has a big bad .... and a princess on the front.'

e 'Please be careful! Don't .... off your bicycle!'

3 **What are the extra letters in the sword? Write them in order and find the name of the king of the dead in the next chapter.** _ _ _ _ _

GUESS WHAT

What does Hercules do in the next chapter?
Read the sentences and write *yes* or *no*.

a Hercules finds the god Atlas. Atlas brings Hera's apples to him. ......

b Hercules finds Hera's dragon. He gets on its back and finds Hera's apples. ......

c Hercules goes up into the sky. He asks Zeus for help. ......

d Hercules goes down into the world of the dead. He finds a dog with three heads there. ......

e Hercules marries Princess Admete and he doesn't finish his tasks. ......

f Hercules finishes his tasks and the gods forgive his crime. ......

33

回 CHAPTER 6 回

After many long and **dangerous** days on the road, Hercules arrives at the end of the world. He looks over the wall of Hera's garden and sees the golden apples on a tree. Three young women are sitting under the tree.

'Can I come into your garden?' asks Hercules.

'Are you a god?' they ask.

'No,' says Hercules.

'Sorry, gods only,' they smile.

Just then a dangerous dragon with a hundred heads arrives. 'Bye!' says Hercules.

回

Not far away, Hercules sees the god Atlas. He is **holding** the world on his huge **shoulders**.

'Atlas, how can I get those golden apples?' asks Hercules.

'First, kill the dragon,' says Atlas. 'Then come back and hold the world for me. I can go and get the apples for you easily. Those three young women in the garden are my daughters.'

dangerous that can kill you

hold to take in your hands for a time

shoulder this is between your arm and your neck

Hercules goes and kills the dragon at once. He then takes the world from Atlas and puts it on his shoulders. 'It's very **heavy**,' he thinks. 'I can't hold it for long.'

Soon Atlas comes back with the apples.

'You can have the world again now,' says Hercules.

'No, thank you,' laughs Atlas. 'I don't want to hold it any more. I'm tired of that.'

'All right! But can you take it for one minute?' asks Hercules. 'I want to put it up on my shoulders better. I don't want to drop it!'

So Atlas takes the world on his shoulders again.

'Wonderful! I'm going home now!' says Hercules. 'Thanks for the apples!'

'Come back!' cries Atlas. But Hercules runs away.

<hr>

When Hercules arrives back at Eurystheus's palace with the golden apples, Hera is very angry. 'We must think of one last truly dangerous task for Hercules – a task worse than all the other tasks before it,' she says to the king. 'I know! Let's send him down into the **underworld**. He can bring back King Hades and Queen Persephone's dog, Cerberus. Nobody can get away from that dog alive.'

heavy not easy to hold

underworld the country where dead people live, under our feet

35

At first, Hercules can't find the door to the underworld, but Athena helps him. 'Go down that big hole behind those rocks,' she says.

Hercules goes down the long, dark hole and meets an old man near a river.

'I'm Charon,' says the man. 'I take dead people across the river to the underworld in my long black boat.'

'Take me across too,' says Hercules.

Charon looks carefully at Hercules. 'No,' he says, 'I can't. You're not dead.'

Hercules holds up his sword in front of Charon's face, and he looks angrily at the old man.

'Oh, all right,' says Charon, and he takes Hercules across the river in his boat.

Once Hercules is in the underworld, he walks through its dark streets. Dead and cold white people come and look at his warm pink skin. 'Can you see that? He's alive!' they say.

In the end Hercules arrives at Hades and Persephone's tall, dark palace. He tells them about his twelve tasks.

'Can I take Cerberus with me?' he asks them. 'It's the last of my tasks.'

'Yes, you can,' says King Hades. 'But please bring him back after Eurystheus sees him. He's our guard dog, you know.'

Hercules goes up to Cerberus. He is a huge dog with three heads and snakes all over his body. He runs at Hercules with his three big mouths open. But Hercules is not afraid. He does not run away. He catches Cerberus in his hands.

Then he plays with him, and says nice things to him. In the end, Cerberus is happy to go with him. Not many people are nice to Cerberus, you see.

□

When Hercules walks back into the palace with Cerberus, Eurystheus gets into his jar. 'Aaagh! Take that dangerous dog away from here!' cries Eurystheus. He is very afraid. 'That's it, Hercules! No more tasks. And I never want to see you again!'

□

Hercules takes Cerberus back to the underworld. Then he goes to the priestess at Delphi, and falls at her feet. 'My twelve tasks are over,' he says. 'Can the gods forgive me now for my crime?'

'Yes,' says the priestess. 'The gods forgive you. You are only half a god now, but when your time comes to die, you can go and live in the sky with your father, Zeus. Then you can be truly a god and never die.'

'Me? A god?' says Hercules. 'How can that be?' He is very surprised.

□

But through the years, everybody learns about Hercules – the strongest man in the world – and his twelve tasks. No one forgets his story once they hear it. You are reading it today. And so, you can see, it is true – in the end, Hercules never dies.

READING CHECK

Put these sentences in the correct order. Number them 1–8.

a ☐ Hercules goes across to the underworld in a  .

b ☐ Atlas gets the  for Hercules.

c ☐ The priestess at Delphi tells Hercules, 'You are a half  '.

d ☐ Hercules catches  and takes him to Eurystheus.

e ☐ Atlas gives the  to Hercules. Hercules puts it on his strong shoulders.

f ☐ Hercules goes to Hera's  at the end of the world.

g ☐ Eurystheus is  when he sees Cerberus and he sends Hercules away.

h ☐ Hercules gives the world back to  and takes the apples to Eurystheus.

WORD WORK

Use the words in the tree to complete the sentences.

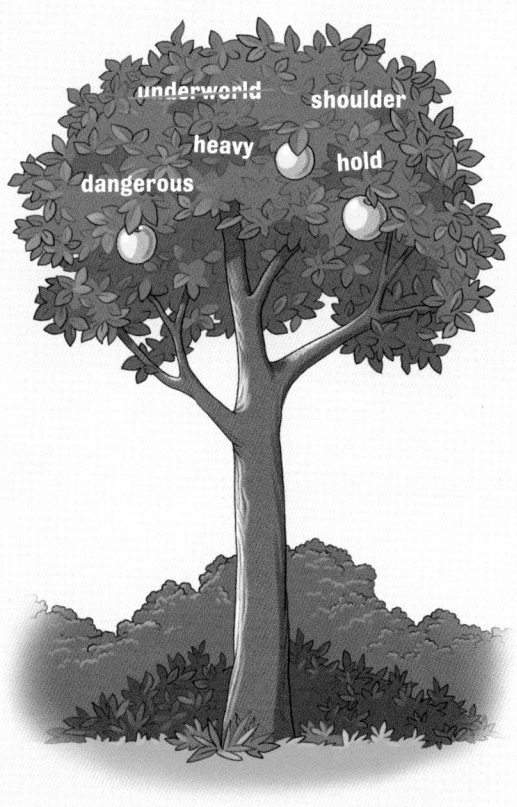

a 'The end of the film is very exciting. He goes down into the .underworld. and brings back his dead wife.'

b 'Can you .... my coat for me for a minute? I need to make a phone call.'

c 'Please don't drop that big .... table on my foot!'

d 'It can be very .... to go up that big mountain when there's a lot of snow on it.'

e 'That's my friend near the window. She's got a red bag over her ....'

GUESS WHAT

What happens to Hercules after the end of the story? Choose from these ideas or add your own.

a ☐ Hercules is very happy to finish the tasks. He goes to different countries on the boat *The Argo*.

b ☐ Hercules is very tired after his tasks so he stays in bed for a year.

c ☐ Hercules is angry with Eurystheus so he goes back to the palace and fights him.

d ☐ Hercules marries the priestess at Delphi and they have a lot of children.

e ☐ The goddess Hera makes Hercules kill his best friend. He then needs to do tasks for Queen Omphale.

f ☐ Hercules chases and catches the goddess Hera. The god Zeus helps him.

g ☐ ....

h ☐ ....

Project A *Monsters*

1 Look at the picture of the Hydra. Read the description and find seven more mistakes.

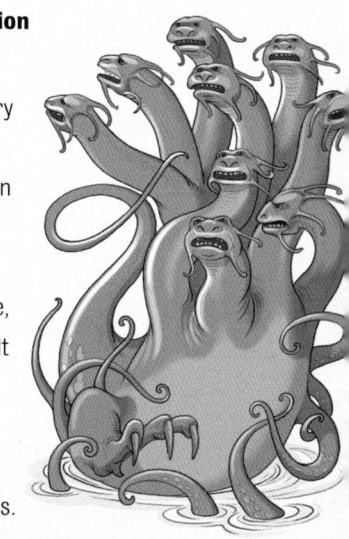

The Hydra is a ~~small~~ *big* monster with seven heads. On every head, there are three angry blue eyes and a hungry mouth. It has a big body and a long tail. Its skin is brown in colour.

The Hydra lives in the cold waters of the Lake of Lerna. When dragons, wild boars or people come near the lake, it quickly kills and eats them with its fourteen mouths. It also likes eating river birds and water snakes.

The Hydra can swim very fast in the water and it can catch things easily with its three long arms. It can also see things from far away because it has twenty-one eyes.

2 Read the description of the Gryphon. Tick the correct picture below. Then use the words in the box to complete the description of the Gryphon.

body   catch   ears   eating   mountain   wings

a ☐

b ☐

c ☐

d ☐

The Gryphon is a brown and white monster with the head of a bird and the **a** .... and tail of a lion. It has two huge **b** .... It can fly up into the sky with those On the top of its head there are two big **c** .... It can hear very well with those. It has four strong legs. Its front two legs are like a bird's and are very dangerous.

At night the Gryphon lives in a dark hole in the side of a **d** .... By day it flies down to the hills and villages and looks for food. It likes **e** .... deer, cows and small horses.

The Gryphon never gets tired and it can fly up in the sky for hours and hours. It can also come down suddenly and **f** .... things in its huge claws.

6 Now draw and write about your own monster. Make notes in the table below and use some of the words with pictures to help you. Then write your description.

Name of monster	
Description	
Where it lives	
What it eats	
What it can do	

Use these words to help you.

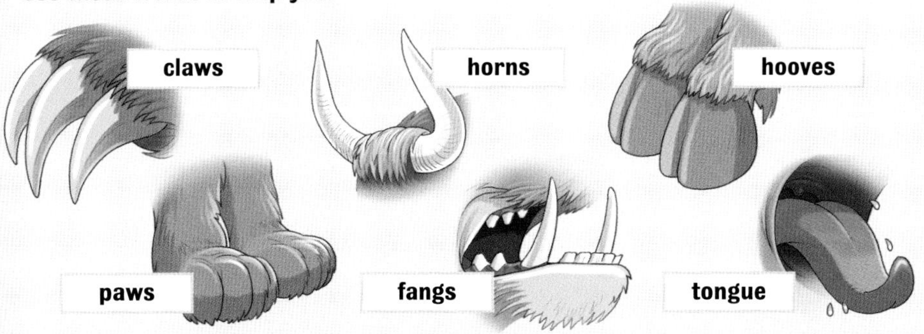

claws

horns

hooves

paws

fangs

tongue

41

Project B — *Interview with a character*

1 Read this interview with Hercules on a chat show. Complete the conversation with these questions.

And what do you like doing all day?

What do you think of him?

And where do you feel happiest?

And what do you want to do in the future?

Who is your father?

And which of the gods do you like?

Interviewer: Ladies and gentlemen, our next guest is the superhero Hercules! Welcome to the show, Hercules.

Hercules: Thank you.

Interviewer: Can I ask you an important question first?

Hercules: Yes, of course.

Interviewer: a ....

Hercules: Well, not many people know this, but Zeus is my father.

Interviewer: I see. b ....

Hercules: Well, I like killing dangerous monsters, catching wonderful animals, and visiting different countries.

Interviewer: c ....

Hercules: In the mountains. It's beautiful there.

Interviewer: OK. Now what about King Eurystheus? d ....

Hercules: I work for him, but I don't like him. He laughs at me all the time.

Interviewer: Oh dear. e ....

Hercules: I like Zeus, of course, and the goddess Athena. She always helps me, you see. I don't like Zeus's wife, Hera. And she doesn't like me.

Interviewer: I see. f ....

Hercules: When I stop working for Eurystheus, I want to go round the world and look for a beautiful woman to marry.

Interviewer: Well, good luck, Hercules! And thanks for coming on the show today.

PROJECTS

**2 Read this interview with Hera on a chat show. Complete the conversation with
sentences from the box. (There are some extra sentences.)**

> I don't like that man or his mother, Alcmene.　　I eat 'ambrosia' and I drink 'nectar'.
>
> I like finding and catching my enemies.　　I live on Olympus, the mountain of the gods.
>
> I want to find and kill Hercules.　　In my beautiful garden at the end of the world.
>
> My husband is the god Zeus – the king of all the gods.
>
> My mother was Rhea and Kronos was my father.
>
> Well, I love my son, Ares, and daughter, Hebe.

Interviewer:　Ladies and gentlemen, this week our guest is the goddess Hera! Welcome Hera – we're lucky to have you here today.

Hera:　Yes, you *are* lucky. I don't usually come on chat shows, you know. And call me *Goddess* Hera, thank you very much.

Interviewer:　Yes … yes. Now, first of all, Goddess Hera, tell us all about your family. Who's your husband?

Hera:　**a** .... Everybody knows that.

Interviewer:　Of course. Er … and what do you like doing?

Hera:　**b** ....

Interviewer:　Oh, I see. Now tell me: where do you feel happiest?

Hera:　**c** ....

Interviewer:　Oh, I know it. It has a tree in it with lots of golden apples on it.

Hera:　Don't talk to me about those apples!

Interviewer:　Sorry. Let's move on to my next question. What do you think of Hercules?

Hera:　**d** Hercules! ....

Interviewer:　Oh dear. And which of the gods do you like?

Hera:　**e** .... But I don't like any of the other gods or goddesses on Olympus.

Interviewer:　And now my last question. What do you want to do in the future?

Hera:　**f** ....

Interviewer:　I see. That's …interesting. Well, thank you very much, Hera … that's *Goddess* Hera, of course. Goodbye and good night, everybody!

3 Imagine you are the interviewer on a chat show. Write questions to ask one of these people. Work with a partner. Ask and answer the questions. Use the information below to help you.

Name	King Hades
Family	wife – the goddess Persephone
Likes	going for walks with Cerberus the dog
Feels happiest	next to the dark river – The Styx – in the underworld
Friend	Charon – the boat man
Favourite god or goddess	his brother, the sea god Poseidon
Future	wants to go on a warm holiday in the sun

Name	Queen Hippolyta
Family	father – Ares, the god of war
Likes	walking, running, shooting arrows
Feels happiest	under the trees in the country of the Amazons
Friend	her sister, Melanippe – she's an Amazon guard
Favourite god or goddess	Athena, the goddess of wisdom
Future	wants to find a strong husband

GRAMMAR CHECK

Possessive adjectives

We use the possessive adjectives my, his, her, its, our, your and their to show that somebody or something belongs to somebody, when we do not use the owner's name.

Alcmene is Hercules's mother. = Alcmene is his mother.

He can bring back the King and Queen's dog, Cerberus. = He can bring back their dog, Cerberus.

The deer's name was Cerynitis. = Its name was Cerynitis.

Possessive adjectives go in front of the noun.

I = my	*she = her*	*we = our*	*they = their*
he = his	*it = its*	*you = your*	

1 Write possessive adjectives for the underlined words.

her	his	its	my	our	their	your

a <u>Eurystheus's</u> jar   ...his... jar

b <u>The Hydra's</u> heads   .... heads

c <u>Hippolyta's</u> belt   .... belt

d <u>Hades and Persephone's</u> dog   .... dog

e <u>My son and Zeus's</u> son   .... son

f '<u>Hercules's</u> cousin,' says Hercules. .... cousin

g '<u>Megara's</u> children,' Hercules tells Megara. .... children

2 Complete the sentences with the correct possessive adjectives.

a 'Those are ...my... snakes!' cries Hera.

b Hercules kills .... wife and .... sons.

c Hercules kills the big lion and wears .... skin.

d Athena says to Hercules, 'I come from .... father, Zeus.'

e Artemis has a golden deer. Hercules must catch .... deer for .... third task.

f Diomedes says, '............ horses are hungry!'

g Augeas has many bulls, but .... stables are very dirty.

h The Amazons love .... queen, Hippolyta.

45

GRAMMAR CHECK

Questions with question words, or 'information questions'

We use question words – such as who, what, why, where, when, how, how long, how many – in information questions. We answer these questions by giving information.

Who is Athena?	*Athena is a goddess.*
Where does the story happen?	*The story happens in Greece.*
How many tasks does Hercules have?	*Hercules has twelve tasks.*

When we ask a question with why, the answer has the word because.

Why can't Hercules talk to Iolaus?   *Because he's going to the Lake of Lerna.*

3 Look at the underlined words. Change each sentence to an information question. Use question words.

a .Why does the priestess give twelve tasks
    .to Hercules...?

The priestess gives twelve tasks to Hercules <u>because he kills his wife and sons</u>.

b ....?

The Hydra lives <u>in the Lake of Lerna</u>.

c ....?

Athena gives <u>a large metal rattle</u> to Hercules.

d ....?

Hercules goes to Geryon's country <u>by boat</u>.

e ....?

<u>Geryon</u> has beautiful red cows.

f ....?

Geryon has <u>three</u> heads.

g ....?

Hercules stays on the white bull's back <u>for two days</u>.

h ....?

The gods forgive Hercules <u>after he finishes his last task</u>.

GRAMMAR CHECK

Superlative adjectives

We add –est to make the superlative form of most short adjectives.

tall   *the tallest*

When adjectives finish in e, we add –st.

nice   *the nicest*

When adjectives finish in a short vowel + a single consonant, we double the final consonant and add –est.

big   *the biggest*

When adjectives finish in a consonant + y, we change y to i and add –est.

hungry   *the hungriest*

With adjectives with two or more syllables, we put the most before the adjective.

interesting *the most interesting*

Some adjectives have an irregular superlative form.

good   *the best*

bad   *the worst*

1 Complete the sentences with superlative adjectives.

a Hercules is ...the strongest... (strong) man in the world.

b Alcmene is .... (beautiful) princess in Greece.

c Iolaus is .... (good) of all of Hercules's cousins.

d Athena is .... (nice) goddess of them all.

e Artemis's deer is .... (fast) deer in the world.

f Zeus is .... (important) god of them all.

g King Augeas's stables are .... (dirty) stables in Greece.

h Eurystheus is .... (bad) king in Greece.

i Geryon's cows are .... (red) and .... (fat) cows in the world.

j Hera is .... (angry) goddess of them all.

GRAMMAR CHECK

Short answers

We use short answers to reply to Yes/No questions. In a short answer, we re-use the auxiliary verb or the verb be from the question.

Is it Hera's garden? Yes, it is.

We use the same pronoun in the short answer as in the question.

Does it have an apple tree in it? Yes, it does.

5 **Write short answers for the questions about the picture.**

a Is there a dragon in the garden? ...Yes, there is...

b Does it have lots of heads? ....

c Are there three women in the garden? ....

d Are they wearing dresses? ....

e Are they wearing hats? ....

f Does the garden have a wall? ....

g Is the wall black? ....

h Are there any chairs in the garden? ....

i Is the god Atlas standing in the garden? ....

j Is Hercules in the garden? ....

k Are there golden apples on the tree? ....

l Is there a dog in the garden? ....

m Is the sky blue? ....

n Does the garden have a house in it? ....

GRAMMAR

GRAMMAR CHECK

To + infinitive or –ing form verb

After the verbs *finish*, *go*, *like*, *love*, and *stop*, we use verb + –ing.

I love reading.

After the verbs *forget*, *learn*, *need*, *remember*, *want*, and *would like*, we use to + infinitive.

I'd like to read that book.

We can use to + infinitive or verb + –ing after *begin* and *like*.

Hera begins to feel angry.   *Hera begins feeling angry.*

Eurystheus doesn't like to look at the cows.   *Eurystheus doesn't like looking at the cows.*

6 **Complete these sentences. Use the** ***to + infinitive*** **or** ***–ing*** **form of the verbs in brackets.**

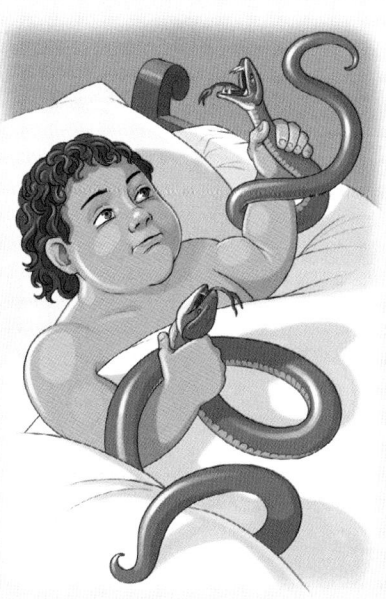

a Hercules learns ...*to kill*... (kill) when he's a little boy.

b He loves .... (live) in the country.

c He begins .... (work) for King Eurystheus when he leaves Delphi.

d Zeus wants .... (help) Hercules.

e Hercules needs .... (do) twelve tasks for the gods to forgive him.

f He doesn't like .... (be) nice to Eurystheus.

g Iolaus likes .... (fight) the Hydra with Hercules.

h Hercules remembers .... (ask) Athena for her help at Lake Stymphalus.

i Princess Admete would like .... (have) Hippolyta's belt.

j Hercules doesn't want .... (kill) Hippolyta.

k Atlas stops .... (hold) the world for a time when Hercules takes it from him.

l Hercules doesn't forget .... (take) Cerberus back to the underworld.

m He finishes .... (work) for Eurystheus when he does all of his tasks.

49

GRAMMAR CHECK

Articles: a/an, the

We use the indefinite article a / an when we talk about singular nouns, when it is not clear which of several things we may mean. We use a in front of a word that begins with a consonant and an in front of a word that begins with a vowel or vowel sound.

Zeus is a Greek god.   *It is an old story.*

We use the definite article the when we talk about singular and plural nouns, when it is clear which of several things we mean.

Many people know story.   *The lions live in the hills.*

7 Complete the sentences with *a/an*, or *the*.

a ....The..... priestess at Delphi helps Hercules.

b .... king has .... big brown jar. He gets into .... jar when he's afraid.

c .... Hydra lives in .... lake. .... lake is called .... Lake of Lerna.

d .... goddess Artemis has .... expensive golden deer. Hercules catches .... deer near .... lake.

e Eurystheus has .... daughter, Princess Admete. .... princess always wants things.

f There's .... river near Augeas's dirty stables. Hercules uses .... river to clean .... stables.

g Athena arrives with .... metal rattle. She gives .... rattle to Hercules.

h Hercules puts some fire onto .... arrow and shoots .... arrow.

i Queen Hippolyta is .... Amazon. .... Amazons are big strong women.

GRAMMAR CHECK

Present Continuous: affirmative and negative

We use the Present Continuous to talk about things happening now.

Hercules is going to Crete.   *You are reading Hercules's story today.*

We make the Present Continuous affirmative with the verb be + the –ing form
of the verb.

Queen Hippolyta is wearing a golden belt.   *The big black birds are killing all the cows.*

We put n't (not) with the verb be to make the Present Continuous negative.

Hercules isn't holding the world on his shoulders.

The birds aren't staying in the trees.

**Look at the picture and complete the text. Use the Present Continuous form of the
verbs in brackets.**

Ganymede **a** ..is. holding. (hold) a bottle and he **b** .... (give) drinks to
everybody. Zeus **c** .... (sit) on his big chair. He **d** .... (drink).
Hades and Persephone **e** .... (come) through the door. They
f .... (not run). Hercules and Athena **g** .... (sit) near the fire.
Hercules **h** .... (eat) something. Athena **i** .... (smile) and she
j ....(hold) a drink. Hera **k** .... (put) a little snake in Athena's
drink. She **l** ....(not smile). She **m** .... (look) at Hercules and she's
angry. Atlas **n** .... (stand) on one leg on the table. He **o** .... (catch)
the world. Artemis **p** .... (shoot) a bird through the window.

DOMINOES Your Choice

Read *Dominoes* for pleasure, or to develop language skills. It's your choice.

Each *Domino* reader includes:
- a good story to enjoy
- integrated activities to develop reading skills and increase vocabulary
- task-based projects – perfect for CEFR portfolios
- contextualized grammar activities

Each *Domino* pack contains a reader, and an excitingly dramatized audio recording of the story

If you liked this *Domino*, read these:

Blackbeard
Retold by John Escott

The year is 1717. It is a bad time to be the captain of a ship in the Caribbean because of pirates. The most frightening pirate on the sea is Edward Teach, or 'Blackbeard'.

'The Governor of Virginia wants us all dead!' Blackbeard thinks. 'But can he kill me – the most famous pirate in the Caribbean? No!' This is his story…

William Tell and Other Stories
Retold by John Escott

'The men and the women in this book – William Tell, Tom Blood, Lord Bao, King Matthias, Johnny Appleseed, and Lady Godiva – are all real people from history.

But every time someone tells an old story, they change things in it, to make them bigger, better, and more exciting. So what is true in this book and what is not? Read all six of the stories, and see what you think.

	CEFR	Cambridge Exams	IELTS	TOEFL iBT	TOEIC
Level 3	B1	PET	4.0	57-86	550
Level 2	A2–B1	KET-PET	3.0-4.0	–	390
Level 1	A1–A2	YLE Flyers/KET	3.0	–	225
Starter & Quick Starter	A1	YLE Movers	1.0–2.0	–	–

You can find details and a full list of books and teachers' resources on our website:
www.oup.com/elt/gradedreaders